A Little Blue Book

A collection of shades of the color blue in
the form of poetry

Sagnik Das

India | USA | UK

Made with ❤ on the BookLeaf Publishing Platform
www.bookleafpub.in
www.bookleafpub.com

Dedication

This book is dedicated to all those humans out there whose life feels like some shade of blue.

Preface

This collection of poems is the ramblings of a middle aged loner, who despite understanding the inevitable loneliness the future holds, dared to dream, take a step out of his comfort zone, fall in love, had his heart broken and most important of all, never for once regretted any of the decisions. The poems in this book capture the loneliness, the yearnings, the hopes, the dreams, the dread, the chaos, the misery and the quiet acceptance of the inevitability of a man willingly stuck in a place, which is devoid of the human connection. The arrangement of the poems has been done in a way to reflect the chaos of feelings that a solitary soul undergoes when he/she/they witness the ever changing world unfold.

Acknowledgements

This book is dedicated to my parents, who have no idea that I write poetry. To my friends, who know about it a little but could never imagine that I would be able to come up with a book. Lastly, this book is dedicated to a very special person, who gave me the strength to dream, courage to fall in love, the gentlest of touches when my heart got broken and the most fiercest supporter and the most avid reader of my poems. I could have never imagined that I would be writing a poetry book if it was not without the constant and consistent support of this poet, who happens to be my favorite person in the world.

1. Blue window

I will walk by your blue window,
when springs will be dull and colorless.
I will walk by your blue window,
when this city will become a rugged mess.

I will walk by your blue window,
when the songbirds will only sing a melancholy song.
I will walk by your blue window,
when sadness will be perpetual, and nights would be
long.

I will walk by your blue window,
when war planes would paint the streets red.
I will walk by your blue window,
when all the poems of prosperity will be buried dead.

I will walk by your blue window,
when everything we hold dear will be rotten.
I will walk by your blue window,
when all we learnt about love will be forgotten.

Don't wait for me, for I would have already passed by,
Don't long for me, for I would have already been
summoned to die.
Keep me hidden in the sparrow's nest, where hope
begins to grow.
For I shall always remain a memory, you saw from your
blue window.

2. 36th Street Irish Bar

The cheap bourbon bottle in the corner,
two shots and two beers, always the order.
We left the cold evenings outside the door,
drew the world we could make on the floor.
You taught me how to make love with music,
The New York crowd never made us sick.
So many drunk nights with you left a scar,
I still imagine you at the 36th street Irish bar.

All that was of you to miss, I think I would,
all that was of you to dismiss, I think I could.
I loved you while sitting alone at the Square,
I loved you the same at the Coney Island fair
When you were with me, I liked to be found,
at the top of the Rock or in the underground.
So many drunk nights with you left a scar,
I still imagine you at the 36th street Irish bar.

Reality never seems to me as a real option,
I find solace when I drink without caution.

Whiskey don't taste the same nowadays,
without your perfume and your embraces.
Further I move away from your memories,
the closer I get to states of cruel reveries.
So many drunk nights with you left a scar,
I still imagine you at the 36th street Irish bar.

3. In a parallel universe

The rain is back outside my windows
and it's pouring inside my room too.
The leftover shadows you left behind,
linger on forever inside my wasted heart.
I wish I could give you a bright, sunny day,
'cause that's all I always wanted to do.
But the pile of mess that my life has been,
is all I can pass on to your coveted heart.
In a parallel universe, when its spring,
I would give you the colors of cherry.
In a parallel universe, when its spring,
I would give you a long sunset.
In a parallel universe, when its spring,
I would love you, the way I am supposed to,
In every universe and the next.

4. She was born in war

She was born in war.
Her hair hid the bombs,
Her breasts borne the wounds.
Her eyes held the mother's tears.
For, she was born in war,
and her heart never gave her peace.

She was born in war.
Mercenaries raped her soul,
Weapons of mass destruction ravaged her being.
Her hands held the corpse left by love.
For she was born in war,
and her affection couldn't heal her world.

Now she has become war.
Her wrath will be unforgiving.
Her retribution will be catastrophic.
Her vengeance will burn like hellfire.
For she was born in war,
and her justice will be too much to bear for this society.

5. Love trickling down the veins

Dark walls reflecting a morbid light,
while loneliness slithers silently.
No respite from this tragedy on sight,
as I tie to my neck, the rope willingly.

There is no future, there is no paradise,
in this labyrinth of distant memories.
Winter's perpetual and the sun would never rise,
only pain and death fill up my reveries.

The blade touches the skin of my soul,
as I see the love trickle down my veins.
Misery and dread have claimed its toll,
as the dead body drenches in the December rain.

The house once was filled with her smile,
The rooms smelled like her favorite perfume.
Now there's only desolation for mile after mile,
as I silently wait for my impending doom.

6. A pauper

I am a pauper when it comes to love.
No rainbows in my skies to lend,
nor a love song for the hearts to mend.
Only a rainy evening outside my door,
or a broken-down soul on the bathroom floor.
Is all that I could offer as a lover's gift.
'cause I am a pauper when it comes to love,
while you offer me an ocean as vast as the skies above.

I am a pauper when it comes to love.
Not a single night filled with the joys of spring,
nor a summer breeze that the migrant birds bring.
I could only offer a morbid conversation about the dead,
stories of decay written on the walls with lead.
Is all that I could offer as a wedding vow.
'cause I am pauper when it comes to love,
while you offer me a soul as pure as the white dove.

7. Revolution will be her grace

She keeps all her dreams in a box,
hidden from the prying eyes of society.
Monsters that creep out from underneath the rocks,
threatening her to live a life of twisted propriety.

Her flesh is devoured, her soul vandalized,
with vile words and menacing glances.
Terrifying norms that are institutionalized,
keeps her from flying and taking her chances.

Walls of judgement crashes upon her garden,
destroying all the flowers she had sown.
Rituals of men devoid of any pardon,
abandons her in a crowd, but all alone.

A day will come, when she will burn like the sun,
seething with the vengeance of an injured tigress.
That day even the Gods will have to hide and run,

for she is a woman, and revolution will always be her
grace.

8. Lonely man with a fedora hat

Christmas glows on the fifth avenue,
a resting place for so many dreams.
As a lonely man, with a fedora hat,
I get lost within the bustling lanes of lower east side,
and reminisce your voice within a million screams.

Lives are counted with whiskey glasses,
while chasing ghosts in a Manhattan bar.
The whole of New York looks like you tonight.
I wish you were here in the city,
and not calling from a dimension so far.

Hanging from the Brooklyn Bridge rails,
souls searching for a chance to lose or gain.
As a lonely man, with a fedora hat,
I look for your footsteps on the brick roads of Dumbo,
and hear your name being repeated by the rain.

Central Park is where they found my body,

searching for poets in the freezing lake.
The whole of New York looks like you tonight.
I wish you were here in the city,
for my heart was always yours to take.

9. I will remember you

Last evening i stopped at an old gas station on the
interstate,
The failing light of the sun on the horizon reminded me
of your going away.
An inevitability, not a grand gesture that happened
sooner than late,
like a prophecy foretold by the failed poets disguised in
suits of clay.
The cigarette tasted different, like your effervescent soul,
deadly but addictive.
Like the nights you spent unhinged and vulnerable in
my shoddy room.
Crawling on the empty and endless sky were your
images that remain afflictive.
Deserted and forgotten Christmas trees like my heart
waited for the impending doom.
Distant headlights seemed like your eyes that I saw
when we met for the first time,
From a distance, not too close, but forever warning of my
inescapable wither.

The cold wind from the north filled my world with a
song without a reason or rhyme.
It had your voice when you said you only wished we
could be together.

I will remember you with the yellow autumn trees,
I will remember you with a new lover's unease.
I will remember you with the adventure of old dirt
roads.
I will remember you with the strings of a guitar about to
corrode.
I will remember you in the decadence of an old church
tower.
I will remember you in the songs of revolution sang
against power.
I will remember you in the freshly brewed coffee of a
highway diner.
I will remember you in the country music of the rust belt
miner.
I will remember you as much as my failing memory
allows.
I will remember you in the words of other's wedding
vows.

10. Ghostly winds of a lonely spring

The ghostly winds of a lonely spring,
What new heartbreaks did you now bring?
Your songs always play the melancholy tunes,
of lovers and poets and of deserts and dunes.
You bring forth a longing for that special night,
like a mother's embrace or a glowing warm light.

The ghostly winds of a lonely spring,
What new heartbreaks did you bring?
Have you brought news of my romance's demise,
or would a budding new intimacy arise?
You seize the hearts of the young and the old,
whisper the stories of love, that remains untold.

The ghostly winds of a lonely spring,
What new heartbreaks did you bring?
Have you brought back the letters of my sweetheart,
the evenings of fondness we couldn't stay apart?

You ran like a free spirit through her flowing hair,
as I kept on her feet my life, all vulnerable and bare.

11. A city burdened by your absence

Neon reflections on my car windows,
highlights the ancient lives of ghosts,
of a city burdened by your absence.
Forgotten children of forlorn skid rows,
crying out to their unwelcoming hosts,
pleading for a glimpse of your innocence.

Under the dim lights of a shady neighborhood,
abandoned flowers seek the company of lost men,
secretly wishing to hold on to the hope you inspired.
Disillusioned rebels, against injustice who stood,
poets who would write sonnets about the rain,
all lie in the purgatory of your memories, tired.

Fungus infested cafes and dance halls,
where loneliness is the only feeling that survives,
yearns for your return to feel the warmth of your light.
Theater of dreams, where curtains no longer fall,
attracts moans, groans and terribly long sighs,

begs to the vengeful gods for a moment of your sight.

Since the day you walked out of the city we built,
It has not seen a single day of spring.
Since the day you abandoned the streets we designed,
it has not heard a single sparrow sing.
Since the day you last touched my soul,
I ceased to exist as a living human being.

12. The monsters that hide inside my head

The monsters that hide inside my head,
who are still alive when I wished they were dead.
Ravaging my soul, feasting on my joys,
like my heart is their playground and emotions are just
toys.
Burning me from the inside, turning everything to dust,
All my cherished memories are slowly turning into rust.
Cannot seem to escape, cannot seem to hide,
from the pangs of overwhelming sorrow's tide.
The monsters that hide inside my head,
who are still alive when I wished they were dead.

The monsters that hide inside my head,
who are still alive when I wished they were dead.
They make a mockery of my life and my love,
paints with blood the wings of the white dove.
Insanity they trigger and misery they instigate,
I try to catch the train, but I am always late.
Craving for some help I reach out to the unknown,

Inside me a malignant cancer has grown.
The monster that hides inside my head,
who are still alive when I wished they were dead.

The monsters that hide inside my head,
who are still alive when I wished they were dead.
A day will come when I would see again a bright spring,
when you will be in my arms and the birds will sing.
When the eternal fires that burn will be washed away by
rain,
and the battle will be won by love against all the pain.
Your touch will heal my wounds and my heart,
and the sound of your bangles will tear this wall of
sadness apart.
The monsters that hide inside my head,
I will slay them all and they will be dead.

13. Five dollar solace

It is here that solace was sold.
Five dollars for a glass of false promises.
As the evening sun breathed fire,
broken souls gathered for their funerals.

A doctor, a soldier, a failed actor.
Nameless and faceless entities.
I sat in silence in the dark corner,
dreaming of a home that didn't exist.

It is here that I wove my many miseries.
For I am a true genius of misfortunes.
From depressed drunkards to disappointed poets,
I have worn many faces under these dim lights.

Non-resident alien they asked?
Resident alien I snapped back.
No matter the shade of my skin,
This is where I understood true loneliness.

A city that offered me a chance.
But secretly it took away my essence.
Every time I would rediscover what I lost,
It is here that I bought the five dollar solace.

14. What did she feel like?

My friend asked me the other day.
What colour did she feel like?
I answered, like the blue of the Mediterranean bay.

My mother asked me last night.
What do her eyes say?
I answered, they speak of a paradise beyond the fading
light.

My father questioned me one evening.
What does her touch entail?
I answered, they foretell the coming of an eternal
spring.

I stood in front of the mirror and asked myself today.
What emotions does this distance from her invoke?
I answered, laws of physics do not apply to my love, for I
am poet they say.

15. I miss you

I miss you in the long pauses,
in between the ticks of a clock.
I miss you in the revolutionary causes,
that Palestinians write on a rock.

I miss you in the mundane summers,
when the heat kills the joys of light.
I miss you in the beats of a drummer,
whose parades involved the silence of night.

I miss you in the violence of the sea,
bringing ruin to every grain of sand.
I miss you when two birds disagree,
over a crumb of bread, like its land.

I miss you in everything that the universe could conjure,
from the brightest of stars to the darkest of abyss.
I miss you in the pains lovers endure,
for missing you is an eternal bliss.

16. The way you see me

The way you see me,
like a mother looking at her child's eyes,
for the first time underneath heather coloured morning
skies.
Like the ocean that delves deep into the hearts of the
sands,
drawing with it every grain it can grasp on to like it's a
final goodbye.

The way you see me,
like a lonely Bedouin peering into the eyes of a desert
moon,
seeking a path to the lands of the green mountain.
Like an old forgotten road through the woods,
keenly waiting for the sound of a footstep that once
treaded.

The way you see me,
like an aged Indian searching for her lost history in the
blue mountains,

reading every fallen leaf with the unbeatable dedication
of death.
Like the neon lights of a decadent city,
hopelessly waiting for the revival of its former glories.

The way you see me,
a way devoid of prejudice or judgement, with a power of
sight reserved only for the gods.
A way that sings to my soul a lullaby of childhood,
buried deep underneath the miseries of life.
The way you see me, a way only you can see, brings
forth my salvation.

17. A yellow canary

The house feels like a hotel room,
where imminent sorrow always looms.
Splitting your heart into parts of two,
one part broken and the other you rue.
All the ghosts of your decadent past,
and the feelings seem to forever last.
You cannot find the light of the exit door,
a proposition to put your body on the floor.

Look to the east on the coming of the light,
you may find me standing within your sight.
I cannot give you the tender warmth of May,
or a field of Tulips where young lovers lay.
I cannot give you a world without violence,
or return you to your age of innocence.
I will be a yellow canary outside the window,
catching drops of your tears as they flow.

18. You will be every revolution

I want to spill the ocean you hold in your longing heart,
split your open skies with the songs of unforgiven
melancholy.
The emptiness that you cover yourself with every day,
trying hard not to break down on the edge of your
being.
I want to grab all the springs of your happy childhood,
and paint the grey of all the rooms of your blessed heart.
I want to reclaim the city that holds the best versions of
you,
and fight a war for it till the end of the world.
I want to be a God that gives birth to a new planet,
and be the same old devil to whoever wants to destroy
it.
There's no need for you anymore to search for life in
outer space,
and seek the validation of life from incoherent alien
objects.
In the new world, you will reside in every blade of grass,

every rain drop that washes away all the decadence,
in the forefront of every change that visionaries have
dreamt.
In the new world, you will be every revolution.

19. It is here

I picked the colors you left behind,
on the boulevards of the blind.
Some were black and some were grey,
but most were like a brilliant day.
Followed the flowers that slipped from your hair,
through the meadows, islands and where nobody dares.

Ancient cities on every inch of your skin,
crumbled down from their own sin.
You stood alone against the tempest,
while giving my heart a home to rest.
In your embrace I find a night so divine,
cool as a spring breeze, tastes like moonshine.

You carry the children of my favorite dreams,
of a house in a valley where the sunlight gleams.
Footsteps of your damaged and tired feet,
lands on my garden, where oceans meet.
It is here, where I want you to be my forever,
it is here, where tragedy would deny us never.

It is here, where I want to be buried, underneath your
sky,
it is here, where the lovers of Greek tragedies lie.

20. Turn off the light

Concrete trees and plastic cloud,
And deserted children screaming loud.
The air is filled with soot and smoke.
Choirs singing carols while they choke.
Parade for the one's with horrible deaths,
Newborns drowning, gasping for breath.
That's what is left of my city tonight.
Since you decided to turn off the light.

The barrel of the gun plays a seductive tune.
Blade of the knife looks pretty like a full moon.
Crimson will splatter like art on my wall.
I witness alone as my dreams fall.
A star dies with a deafening sound.
The broken body hits the bloodied ground.
That's what is left of my city tonight.
Since you decided to turn off the light.

21. Unlove you

I have travelled to the world's end,
to unnamed islands, where the rivers bend.
I have not found an answer to my question true.
I still haven't learned to unlove you.

I spoke to many people, all great minds,
geniuses and poets, of many different kinds.
With all their wisdom, my knowledge didn't grew.
I still haven't learned to unlove you.

I appealed to the mighty and to the weak,
heard many philosophers and the devils speak.
I tried to listen to the northern winds as they blew.
I still haven't learned to unlove you.

I stood in in front of the mirror to ask the reflection,
the same question that has caused all my affliction.
Finally, I had my answer and a realization too.
I never actually wanted to unlove you.

www.ingramcontent.com/pod-product-compliance
Lightning Source LLC
LaVergne TN
LVHW010926200726
843509LV00013B/2090